For Good Luck!

by Katrina Gold
Illustrated by Wednesday Kirwan

Glenview, Illinois • Boston, Massachusetts • Chandler, Arizona
Upper Saddle River, New Jersey

David

Lyn

It is a rainy day.
David and Lyn have to stay inside.
Mom has an idea!

Mom

"Let's look in the memory box!"
says Mom.
"I keep treasures in the box."
Mom tells a story about the treasures.

Mom takes out the treasures.
Lyn looks at a red box.
David looks at a small bag.

box

bag

"Is this box for earrings?" asks Lyn.
"Yes, it is for the earrings I am wearing," says Mom.
"Tell us the story about the earrings again!" says Lyn.

earring

"Your grandfather gave these earrings to your grandmother," says Mom.
"This happened long ago in China. Your grandfather said they were for good luck."

"I was very unhappy when I left China,"
says Mom.
"Grandma gave me the earrings.
I felt better. One day I will give them to
you, Lyn."

In the bag is a jade stone.
"This is your grandfather's stone from China," says Mom.
"One day I will give it to you, David."
Lyn and David smile.
Stories about treasures are fun!